BREW IT YOURSELF

BREW IT YOURSELF

A COMPLETE GUIDE TO

THE BREWING OF

BEER, ALE, MEAD & WINE

Leigh P. Beadle

FARRAR, STRAUS AND GIROUX
NEW YORK

CONTENTS

To my wife, Becky, my favorite beer-drinking buddy

ACKNOWLEDGMENT

I would like to express my appreciation to those who have
helped me in developing and refining the procedures used in
this book to brew beers and wines; to the research departments
of breweries and wineries both here and abroad. Thanks are
also due all those who have sampled these beers and wines
without knowing that they were not store-bought, so that I got
a candid opinion on how best to develop the main recipes.

No nation is sober when the dearness of fermented malt drinks substitutes ardent spirits as the common beverage.

Thomas Jefferson

BREW IT YOURSELF

Author's Note

The purpose of this book is to provide you with a complete, easy-to-follow guide to making superior beer and wine in your own home. While there are several publications available from England and Europe on brewing, they tend to emphasize the heavier ales and stouts. This book is unique in that the recipes are more attuned to the American preference for light lager beer. Contrary to popular belief, you can make a delicious, high-quality beer for a total outlay of two hours of your time and an initial cost of less than twenty dollars. This investment will provide you with permanent equipment and enough ingredients to make four cases of rich, refreshing beer. At today's prices for commercial beer, you will more than break even on your first two batches! Thereafter, your cost will come to less than five cents a bottle for American-style lager of premium quality and less than ten cents a bottle for beer that is clearly superior to the finest German imported variety. German and other imported beers sell for up to seventy cents a bottle in the better shops.

The beer or wine you make by using the recipes and procedures in this book will bear little relation to any "home-brew" you may have sampled. The art of making wine at home has advanced so rapidly and become so simplified that procedures being used as recently as 1970 are already outdated. The California wineries are producing a superb variety of economical concentrates for the home wine maker which make it unnecessary to buy expensive bushels of grapes and grape-crushing apparatus. These concentrates are made with the *vinifera* wine grapes and they produce a superior wine at a cost of less than fifty cents a bottle. As you can see, this is one hobby that will save you money. The same equipment can be used to make beer or wine, and this book provides information on where to obtain all supplies.

Our procedures for making beer and wine are scientific, and factors that might cause variations in quality from batch to batch have been eliminated. Since fermentation is a natural process, you will be able to produce the highest-quality beer and wine on your first attempt simply by following the instructions closely. The equipment for making beer and wine is compact and convenient. All you will need is space enough for your fermentation vessel, which takes up no more room than a wastebasket.

Glossary of Brewing Terms

ALE
A fermented malt beverage in which top-fermenting yeast is used to carry out the fermentation.

ANAEROBIC FERMENTATION
Method of fermentation whereby air is prevented from coming into contact with the brew.

BARLEY
A grain from which malt is extracted for beermaking.

BREW
A synonym for beer and ale and other beverages that undergo fermentation.

BREWERS' YEAST
A type of yeast, *Saccharomyces cerevisiae,* which has been cultured specifically for brewing beer.

BREWING SALT
A yeast nutrient containing the necessary vitamins and minerals to insure a healthy ferment.

CARBON DIOXIDE
The gas produced by the action of yeast during fermentation.

CARBOY
A closed container used to insure an anaerobic fermentation. The secondary fermenter.

DEXTROSE
A basic sugar, also known as corn sugar. Sometimes used as a substitute for malt in brewing.

FERMENTATION
Process by which yeast acts on sugar to convert it to carbon dioxide gas and alcohol in approximately equal amounts.

FERMENTATION LOCK
A device to insure that carbon dioxide gas can escape from the carboy without allowing air to enter.

FININGS
Substance used to clear and settle beer and wine; forms a slight colloid solution in the brew. Generally gelatin.

GELATIN
See FININGS.

HEAD
The foamy top on all high-quality beers.

HEADING LIQUID
A liquid used by some brewers to put an artificial head on beer when insufficient malt is used to produce a genuine head. Highly undesirable among professional brewers of quality beer.

HOPS
An herb used to impart the characteristic bitter taste to beer and ale.

HYDROMETER
Device used by brewers to measure the amount of unfermented sugars remaining in the beer mix.

INVERT SUGAR
Similar to dextrose.

KILN
Large drum used to dry and warm barley malt.

LAGER
From the German word meaning "to store." A lager beer is one which has been aged in tanks for a period of time.

LEES
Sediment that accumulates above the yeast layer during wine fermentation. Mostly composed of fruit pulp.

MALT
Sugar formed from the starches inside the barley husk.

MALTOSE
Malt sugar which can be converted to alcohol and carbon dioxide gas by the action of the yeast.

MUST
The wine mix before yeast has converted the sugars into alcohol.

NATURALLY CONDITIONED BEER
Beer whose carbonation is produced naturally by fermentation in a sealed bottle. It has a much greater character than the bulk-process or nondeposit beers. These latter beers are charged with carbon dioxide gas prior to bottling and make up the vast majority of the world's commercial beers. Home-brewed beer is naturally conditioned.

NUTRIENT
See BREWING SALT.

PRIMARY FERMENTER
Vessel in which the primary, or tumultuous, fermentation takes place.

PRIMING
The addition of a small amount of dissolved household sugar to the beer just prior to bottling, to produce carbonation.

RACKING
Siphoning wine off the yeast and the lees into another container to prevent it from being affected by undesirable flavors.

SACCHAROMYCES CEREVISIAE
Latin name for brewer's yeast.

SACCHAROMYCES ELLIPSOIDEUS
Latin name for wine yeast.

SECONDARY FERMENTER
Vessel in which the secondary fermentation takes place. Also called the carboy.

SIPHONING
Method by which liquid is transferred from one container to another. For siphoning to take place, the pouring end of the hose must be lower than the suction end.

STOUT
A British dark beer that is very heavy. It generally has a high hop concentration, which makes the drink bittersweet. In my opinion, a beverage most favored by those who would relish a castor-oil cocktail.

SUGAR
In brewing, the malt sugar to be fermented.

WORT
The correct term for the beer mix prior to fermentation.

YEAST
The organism that converts sugar to alcohol and carbon dioxide gas during its reproductive cycle.

Background

Beermaking is one of the oldest arts known to man. Man, it is now believed, was brewing beer at the same time that he was learning the rudiments of making bread, for any number of grains which were used to make bread could easily have been transformed into beerlike drinks through the natural process of fermentation. Our earliest evidence indicates that barley malt was used in brewing by the Mesopotamians around 6000 B.C. The Egyptians were known to have practiced the art quite avidly around 2000 B.C. They are believed to have introduced spices and herbs —forerunners of the present-day hops—into their beer to counteract the sweet taste of the malts. From Egypt the Greeks carried the art to Europe, and the Romans learned about beer during their conquest of Greece. It is believed that beer was introduced to England by the Roman armies. Hops came into use in Europe as the main herb to complement the malt flavor, and the use of this bitter herb soon spread to England. Besides adding flavor to the beer, hops also acted as a preservative. The consumption of beer in England during the Middle Ages must have been enormous. Historical documents of the Duke of Lancaster indicate that he provided each of the ladies-in-waiting at his court with eight gallons of beer a week!

The importance of beer to the early colonizers of America is evidenced by the landing of the *Mayflower* at Plymouth Rock in Massachusetts instead of at its original destination in Virginia. In the *Pilgrim Journal* we read, "For we could not now take time for further search or consideration, our victuals being much spent, especially our beere."* Beer was stocked on long ocean voyages because it tended to retain its freshness, due to the preservative qualities of the hops, whereas water soon spoiled. Beer also provided the vitamins and minerals needed to fight diseases such as scurvy, which plagued ocean voyagers. Early colonial governments recognized the healthful qualities of beer. The Virginia Assembly sent a proclamation to new colonists urging them to bring malt with them to "Brewe and drink beere, until their bodies were hardened to the drinking of water." William Penn opened the

---

* Reprinted from the *Encyclopedia Americana* (1967 edition) by permission of the publishers, Grolier Incorporated, New York.

first commercial brewery in Pennsylvania, and George Washington maintained a brewery on his estate at Mount Vernon, where he was known as a master brewer of fine beers.

In the century following the Revolutionary War, a brewhouse was an essential part of the American household and brewing was encouraged by the government. In 1789 James Madison made a motion before the United States House of Representatives that the low duty of eight cents a barrel be placed on malt liquors, so that "this low rate will be such an encouragement as to induce the manufacture of beer in every state of the Union." A specific example of legislation to foster beer drinking in the early days of the republic is found in the Massachusetts Act of 1789, which states that "the wholesome qualities of malt liquors greatly recommend them to general use, as an important means of preserving the health of the citizens of this commonwealth, and of preventing the pernicious effect of spirituous liquors."

Around 1840 the types of beer brewed in this country began to change. Up until that time, the predominant brew was the traditional British-type ale, a strong, heavy, rather bitter drink with a high alcohol content, averaging around eight percent by weight, or higher. With the influx of German immigrants around the middle of the nineteenth century, however, a lighter, much milder beer began to be made here. The Germans set up breweries that made the lighter, milder, bottom-fermenting lagers typical of regions such as Bavaria. After the turn of the century, American tastes favored an even lighter beer.

One good reason for this tendency toward lightness is that the United States has a much warmer climate than Europe and we need a beer that will quench thirst, a beer that can be quaffed in fair quantities, without leaving us drunk in the process. Prohibition was also a factor in our turning to lighter beer. During this period, beer and wine, along with hard liquor, were prohibited, and breweries were forced to turn out a brew called "near beer," a very light beverage that contained less than one half of one percent alcohol by weight. Fortunately for those who prefer real beer, Prohibition ended with the enactment of the Twenty-first Amendment on December 5, 1933. After a long thirteen years ten months nineteen days seventeen hours and thirty-two and one half minutes, Americans could again step up to a bar for a real beer.

I had a discussion recently with an executive of one of the major brewing firms concerning the lightness of American beer. He told me something interesting about the trend to very light, dry beer following World War II. At that time, he said, women throughout the country began drinking beer. Many men were in military service, and with the pay scales at a rather meager level, they had only a limited amount of money to spend on dates when they could get a weekend pass. Most couples could just afford hot dogs and a pitcher of beer on their evenings of wining and dining. For the first time, women drank beer regularly, but they objected to the bitter taste. To make beer more enjoyable to women, then, it became the custom to dilute a pitcher of beer with a glass of ice water, to weaken the taste. After the war, beer became available at the local supermarket, where it was bought for home consumption, instead of at the local tavern. Since it was the women who did the buying, the breweries catered to their taste for the weaker, blander beer they had become accustomed to drinking during the war.

This is certainly a plausible explanation for the popularity in this country of ultra-light beers. We have found, however, that women do not object to the rich, strong taste of beer, only to its bitterness. All the women who have sampled the beer recipes in this book have preferred them to the bland commercial beer. They also appreciate the nonfattening quality of home-brewed beer.

American beers average about 3.5 percent alcohol by weight, although some regional beers and ales go as high as 5.5 percent. (An alcohol content of 3.5 percent by weight means that 3.5 percent of the total weight of the beer is pure alcohol.) They are mostly light in color, very dry, and contain a relatively high degree of carbonation. These characteristics give them their very good thirst-quenching qualities. To attain the dryness common to beer produced in this country, breweries have had to use other grains along with the barley malt in brewing, since barley used alone will give beer a richer, heavier taste. The two most common additional grains are corn and rice, which can also be used by themselves to produce beer. When Columbus first arrived in the New World, he noted that the Indians used corn to brew a drink similar to the English beer. In Japan today, rice is used to brew sake, a drink which we know as rice wine but which is more correctly identified as a noncarbonated rice beer.

In Northern Europe, barley malt is almost exclusively the basic grain in brewing. This gives European beer a richer, malty taste and adds a certain heaviness to it, but it makes it slightly less desirable as a thirst-quencher. The Germans in particular turn out a highly malted beer that has a characteristic sweetness. This sweetness is countered with a higher hop content, which adds bitterness to the brew. Among the most delicious beers available commercially are some of these German imports, known as "Sunday sipping beers"; also, beers imported from Denmark and Holland. These, incidentally, are the pilsener beers that were considered so light around the middle of the last century, so you can imagine the strength of the brews they were drinking in those days! The term "pilsener," which is used to describe the lighter beers, comes from Pilzen, a town in Czechoslovakia, where the Pilzen brewery has been in continuous operation for over eight hundred years. I've sampled some of their beer and it is delicious, with a rich but mellow taste. One reason for this taste is that the hops grown in Czechoslovakia and in Bavaria lack the harsh, bitter taste that is characteristic of the hops grown in Oregon and Washington State and used in many American beers. Andeker beer, which is brewed in this country, contains hops imported from both Czechoslovakia and Bavaria, and this accounts for its sweet, mellow taste. I enjoy Andeker more than any other beer brewed here. With some of the recipes in this book, you can virtually duplicate the flavor of the imported beers if your taste is for the heavier varieties of brew, and at a considerable savings in cost.

It should be noted that the strength of a beer's flavor is not necessarily due to its high alcohol content. At the risk of incurring the wrath of American tourists to Europe who protest to the contrary, continental brews average around five to six percent of alcohol by weight—half again as much as standard American beers, yet far less than the eight to fourteen percent claimed by our more avid quaffers of the continental brews. A word of advice: Your first inclination may be to increase the alcohol content of the beer recipes given in this book, because, "After all, this is the reason for brewing my own beer—to get a more potent brew." Don't stray too far from the recommended level of ingredients, however. There is a definite decrease in the taste and overall quality of beer when the alcohol content goes beyond six percent. The recipes in this book will produce between 4.7 and six percent alcohol, and this is a sufficient amount to complement the taste. The drinking patterns of the British reflect a beer whose alcohol content has been kept within reasonable limits. In England, unlike here, there is a wide choice of popular brews, from the mild and relatively weak pale ales to the strong stouts and porters. The alcohol content ranges from three percent for the lighter ales to nine percent for the heavier stouts. Yet the most popular drink among the British is light ale, for the simple reason that beer drinkers like the taste of beer and therefore like to drink large quantities without becoming intoxicated.

Home-Brewing in the United States

The home-brewing of beer gained a certain degree of popularity in America during Prohibition, when beer could not be purchased, and then during the Depression, when, out of economic necessity, people concocted their own brews. These early attempts at the brewer's art resulted more often than not in a beer that varied from awful all the way up to mediocre. Home-brewers simply did not have access to the proper ingredients and techniques. The standard procedure for making the home-brew of those days was to add one can of malt extract and four or five pounds of sugar to five or six gallons of water. (So far, so good; but after this we go downhill fast.) The final step was the addition of a pack of Fleischmann's yeast, to start the process of fermentation. This it does, but there is one problem. While Fleischmann makes an excellent yeast, it is bakers' yeast and there is a distinct difference between bakers' yeast and brewers' yeast. Bakers' yeast is cultured specifically for use in breadmaking. If used for brewing, it imparts a mustiness to the brew, making it taste yeasty. And because it does not settle out well, it leaves the beer looking cloudy. Do not make this mistake, or your efforts will result in a brew that is not at all satisfactory.

The type of yeast used by brewers is especially cultured for the purpose. It is developed for its ability to promote a vigorous fermentation, its tendency to impart a good lager taste to the beer, and its settling quality, which leaves the beer clear and sparkling. This yeast cannot be bought locally but is readily available through winemakers' supply firms. The scientific name for it is *Saccharomyces cerevisiae*, *"cerevisiae"* being the Latin name for beer. In fact, there are regions in Europe, notably parts of France, where beer is called "cervoise" instead of the more common "bière."

If the early home-brewers in this country had only left out the sugar and used more malt, and if they had had access to brewers' yeast instead of bakers' yeast, the art of brewing your own beer might very well be far more widespread than it is, for, despite Grandpa's allegations to the contrary, his home-brew just didn't make the grade as a fine beer. The comment I get from people who sample my own beer who have tried the former variety is: "This is real beer, I thought you made home-brew!" The difference in terminology is a matter of semantics; the difference in taste is a matter of record.

There are several other factors which affect the quality of the beer you brew. These will be discussed in a later section. They include the quality of the water, the techniques used in mixing the ingredients, and the chemical additives that promote a healthy ferment. Before going into the technique of brewing your own beer, let us consider the methods used by commercial breweries, so we can correlate them with the procedures we shall use in our operation.

How Beer Is Produced Commercially

Four basic ingredients are required to produce lager beer. They are: malt extract, hops, water, and brewers' yeast. A brief description of how commercial breweries produce beer will point out the similarities and the differences between commercial procedures and the steps you will follow as a home-brewer.

The most complicated step for the commercial brewer is the preparation of the malt. This starts with fresh barley, which is a grain much like wheat. First it is cleaned, then saturated with water and placed in huge drums that revolve slowly at a rate of about one turn an hour. Thus the grain is aerated, and allowed to breathe, as it is now coming to life and germinating in the warm drums. Aeration also helps dispel the heat generated by the grain during the germination stage, which is considerable, since the drums may contain as much as 40,000 pounds of malt each. During the germination of the grain, malt is formed inside the husk. After six days, the maximum amount of malt has formed and further growth is ended by kiln-drying the barley seeds at a temperature of about 150° Fahrenheit. At this point, however, not all barley is of high enough quality for brewing beer. If the grains are not of sufficient size to produce a good-quality malt content, this barley is separated and used for distilling into whisky. Grains that are smaller still are used for livestock feed.

Once the barley grains have been kiln-dried, they are hard and brittle, ready for the cracking stage, during which they are cracked open by rollers. This allows the release of the malt when the cracked grains are boiled, during the mashing process. At this point the water and barley grains are kept at a temperature of 153° Fahrenheit for several hours, to set the enzymes and to convert the starches into sugar. The malt has now been completely separated from the spent grains, and hops are added to the malt water. This gives the beer, or "wort," as it is referred to at this stage, its characteristic bitter flavor. The hops also add aroma and impart certain preservative qualities. After the boiling process, when the necessary flavor has been extracted from the hops, and the wort has been sufficiently sterilized, the mixture is allowed to cool to below 70°. Thus the proper temperature is reached for the next stage, which is the addition or "pitching" of the yeast, *Saccharomyces cerevisiae.*

Breweries maintain carefully nurtured yeast colonies in their laboratories, as the quality of beer depends to a large extent on the quality of the yeast. In some breweries, in fact, the cultures are extracted from the bottom of the storage tanks and used in succeeding batches. The yeast, which is in a thick layer, is made up of three sections. The top is composed mainly of dead yeast cells; the bottom, of immature cells; and the middle layer, of the lively, active yeast cells. It is from the middle layer that future yeast cultures are taken.

After the yeast has been pitched, the wort begins the stage of tumultuous fermentation. At this point the yeast is most vigorous and rapidly converts the malt sugars into alcohol and carbon dioxide. It is during the period of rapid fermentation that the sugary wort is transformed into beer. After about a week, the frothing, bubbling fermentation begins to slow down, and the beer is transferred into large storage, or lagering, tanks. The fermentation is then only half complete. It continues at a much slower rate in the tanks for another five to eight weeks. One reason why the rate of fermentation is slower is that most of the sugars have already been converted during the primary fermentation; also, the storage tanks are kept at a temperature of about 33° Fahrenheit, and the cooler the temperature, the slower the yeasts work. It is this cold storage that gives the beer its mellow lager taste. During the lagering of beer, clarifiers (beer finings) are sometimes added to help carry sediment and yeast particles to the bottom and give the beer its clear, sparkling look. Small amounts of gelatin are usually used as finings. They form a colloid solution in the beer which gradually settles to the bottom, carrying all particles with it. The final step in the commercial brewing process is to siphon the beer from the tanks and then to charge it with carbon dioxide gas just before bottling. This gives beer its carbonation, which enhances the taste and produces the characteristic foamy head when it is poured.

Bottled beer may be either regular or "draft." Regular beer is pasteurized at a temperature of 140° F. for twenty minutes before bottling. This is done by passing the beer through heated pipes on the way to the bottles. Beer that is to be draft in bottles is passed through a millipore filter, to prevent yeast from entering the bottle. Both processes prevent continued fermentation in the bottles. The beer has already been charged with the correct amount of carbonation before bottling. If fermentation were to continue inside the sealed bottle, more carbon dioxide would form and the bottle would burst. Draft beer that is to be put into barrels does not have to be filtered, as it is kept under refrigeration to prevent any significant fermentation. Besides, the barrels would withstand a much higher pressure than bottles.

"Draft," with reference to beer, has a different meaning in England and in parts of Europe than it does here. As indicated, we use the term to denote a nonpasteurized beer. On the other side of the ocean, however, draft means noncarbonated. All American beer is well carbonated, but this is not always the case overseas. Some European home-brewing books concentrate on the noncarbonated variety and mention carbonation only as an afterthought. I've tried some of the European "draft" beers, and some of the home recipes for them, and, rest assured, they are as bad as you imagine them to be. They are not included in this book.

Now that we have followed the commercial brewing process, we are ready to consider the method you will use to achieve the same end. You will find our methods just as scientific, though much simpler, and the results quite extraordinary.

Equipment

The equipment needed to brew beer is the same that is used to ferment wine. All necessary equipment can be obtained in one kit through the wine-makers' supply firm listed in the back of this book, and the total outlay for equipment and ingredients should be less than twenty dollars. Considering the cost of store-bought beverages, you will more than break even on your first two batches of beer or your first batch of wine. Thereafter the cost per five-gallon batch of beer will be less than five or ten cents a bottle, depending on the particular recipe you use, and a superb wine will cost less than fifty cents a bottle.

You will need the following equipment:

TWO-GALLON MIXING POT

You may already have one of these in your kitchen, but I would recommend buying a new one to use exclusively for brewing. The one you already own will have trace elements of soap and grease film from previous use, and these two substances, no matter how slight the amounts, should never come into contact with your brewing utensils, as they adversely affect the flavor of beer and wine. The light aluminum pot with wire handles available at any supermarket is quite satisfactory. It costs less than two dollars.

PRIMARY FERMENTER

This is the container in which the primary, or tumultuous, fermentation takes place. There are several different types of containers available. These include earthenware crocks made for the purpose, and large glass bottles—both of which should be avoided. They are heavy, which makes them difficult to work with, and quite breakable, sometimes with painful consequences, as I found out the hard way! They are also difficult to keep clean, and cleanliness, as we shall see in a later section, is paramount in good brewing. A very suitable container of the type I use is offered in the kit supplied by the wine-making supply firm listed on page 103. It is made of an inert plastic which will impart no taste to the brew, and is naturally the correct size.

SECONDARY FERMENTER

This is a plastic "carboy" fitted with a fermentation lock. It is also included in the kit and is of the dimensions required for the recipes listed in this book.

FERMENTATION LOCK

This is purchased with the carboy. It is a device to insure that no air can reach the brew during the secondary fermentation, while at the same time allowing the carbon dioxide to escape. Since beer will spoil just as surely as milk from contact with air, we must insure a totally anaerobic ferment throughout. The lock is simply filled to the lower line with water before the cap is placed on, which then raises the water level, as shown in Figure 3. The gas bubbles out from the pressure within the carboy. On some locks it helps to place a nickel on the cap to give it extra weight. This little trick will make the lock bubble quietly and also makes it unnecessary to refill the lock with water during the two-week fermentation period since it cuts down on water evaporation.

You may ask at this point: "Why use a primary fermenter at all, why not just ferment in the secondary fermenter?" Well, if the foam generated during the first day of fermentation were produced in the confined area of the carboy, it would clog the fermentation lock, seep through it, and make a nice foamy arrangement on the floor, leaving you in danger of having your equipment and yourself removed by your irritated wife.

SIPHONING HOSE

This piece of equipment is needed to transfer the beer between the containers and into the bottles. The brew cannot be poured, as that would upset the yeast sediment and prevent the clarifying of the beer. Figure 5 shows how to cut off the flow to avoid spillage during the bottling process. You may come across siphon sets that have complicated features such as shut-off clamps and automatic siphon pumps. These are expensive, and they are difficult to clean. Also, they do not work as well as the method illustrated. The correct kind of hose with rigid attachment is included in the fermentation kit I've recommended here.

MISCELLANEOUS ITEMS

You will also need the following, which you very likely have around the house already: large roll of Scotch or masking tape; extra-wide box of Saran Wrap; measuring

cup; small saucepan; long plastic spoon; and candy thermometer (optional).

BOTTLES

Using the standard wine-fermentation kit for brewing,
you will need exactly 58 bottles in twelve-ounce size, or
fewer if you use both twelve-ounce and quart-size bottles.
If you use only quart bottles, you will need 22. Do not use
any bottle other than the brown- or green-tinted ones
made specifically for beer. The tint filters out light rays
and is very important. If beer is exposed to light for any
appreciable length of time, the flavor will be affected, due
to photosynthesis. Do not use soft-drink bottles. The necks
are longer than those of beer bottles, and this will hamper
pouring, a technique that is discussed in a later chapter.
The bottles must not have threaded necks either, since a
cap will not form a gas-tight seal over this kind of bottle.
The most satisfactory type is the long-necked, returnable,
twelve-ounce bottle used by taverns. These bottles seem
to have disappeared from grocery shelves in most parts of
the country in the last few years, but I have a feeling they
will be returning soon: throw-away bottles and cans are
a tremendous waste factor and create a litter problem as
thoughtless people dispose of them all over the national
landscape. Your local beer tavern will probably be glad to
sell you the returnable bottles for a dollar a case of twenty-
four. (Make sure you get the carton too.)

You may want to bottle some of your beer in quarts for occasions such as parties when a greater amount is called for. That way, you are reducing the cleaning time, also. Some beer firms still use for their quart sizes bottles with nonthreaded necks. To facilitate storage, get the sturdy twelve-quart carton from your grocer which was originally used to transport the beer. Some of these have handle cutouts and separate sleeves for each bottle.

The expense and trouble of capping your bottles has been eliminated by the invention in England of a sturdy, polyethylene snap-on cap which lasts forever. Fifty-eight of these are included in the fermentation kit. To cap, simply snap on the caps after filling the bottles and tip each bottle upside down once to wet the seal. Then store upright. Rinse each cap in hot water as soon as the bottle is opened, to keep the caps clean.

THE HYDROMETER

Although the procedures suggested in this book will produce in almost all instances the correct amount of carbonation in your beer, there is always the possibility of some variation in the amount of time needed for the beer to completely ferment out. Cold temperatures or a higher or lower than normal mineral content in the water could cause the beer to ferment slower than indicated. If this is the case and you add the priming sugar to beer that still has an excess of malt sugar to ferment, you risk a burst bottle, since fermentation continues after the cap is sealed. With a hydrometer, however, you eliminate the possibility of over- or under-carbonation.

The hydrometer you use should be one designed specifically for fermentation, such as the one included in the fermentation kit suggested. This device simply measures the amount of sugar remaining in the brew to be fermented. Figure 6 will show you how to use it. You can either remove the fermentation lock and insert the hydrometer into the beer after the fifteen-day fermentation, or you can remove some beer by carefully lowering a small juice glass into the beer and fill your testing jar. Either way, there is no danger of spoiling your beer as long as you rinse the hydrometer or glass with water just before use. The air cannot get to the beer, because of the protective layer of carbon dioxide gas resting on the top of the brew. This does not rush out when the lock is removed, since it is heavier than air, and in almost every case the beer will be ready to bottle at this point, anyway. If the beer does need to work out a few more days and you refit the lock, the small amount of air trapped inside will soon be expelled through the lock.

Let's look again at Figure 6. The hydrometer on the left shows a reading of 1.042. This is a standard reading for the beer mix just before the start of fermentation. Water would show a reading of 1.000. Since the beer mix contains sugar, which is heavier than water, the stem will float higher, giving a reading greater than 1.000. The hydrometer on the right shows a typical reading for beer that has aged two weeks in the carboy, just before the priming sugar is added. The reading is 1.010—the final specific gravity of some of the recipes. Each recipe in this book has listed with it a specific gravity which should be attained after fermentation in the carboy. If the reading is greater than this listed specific gravity—for instance, 1.014 instead of 1.010—you would know that the beer should remain in the carboy to ferment for several more days, until it approaches 1.010. It will then be ready to prime with two-fifths of a cup of sugar and bottle. Occasionally you may have a batch that will not quite work down to the final figure even after an additional few days in the carboy. This is sometimes the case when powdered malt is used and is due to the variable amounts of insoluble sugars in the malt, or it may be that you let the temperature of the water rise above 140° F. when mixing the ingredients. If this happens and the fermentation lock is not bubbling at a rate that shows active fermentation, it is safe to prime and bottle. When using the hydrometer, be sure to insert the stem into the jar with a spinning motion, to prevent any bubbles from adhering to the side of the float, as this would give an incorrect reading. The final specific gravity readings in the recipes are already corrected for an assumed room temperature of 70°. The problem of slow fermentation may never arise in your brewing, of course, since the procedures outlined here are very thorough. But this is the extra touch of professionalism in your brewing that will eliminate problems, should they arise. After all, you will want to impress your friends with your newly acquired skill, and they may look askance at your brewing abilities if you walk into the room carrying a sealed bottle of your best brew as if it were a live grenade!

Ingredients

MALT EXTRACT

Most of the recipes in this book call for the use of two types of malt extract, Blue Ribbon hop-flavored, and dried malt extract (unhopped). Do not try to use all of one or the other in the recipes, or the result will be a beer that is either too sweet or too bitter, to the point of being unpalatable. The Blue Ribbon is readily available from most chain supermarkets; a list of those that stock it is included at the end of this section. It comes in Pale Dry, Extra Pale, Light, and Dark. In addition there is Plain extract, which is unhopped. The Pale Dry and Extra Pale are called malt syrup, and the Light, Dark, and Plain are called malt extract on the can. "Syrup" and "extract" mean the same thing; all canned malt extract is in syrup form. The hop flavoring eliminates quite a bit of time and expense in our brewing operation; you won't have to purchase the hops separately and prepare them in the brew. The quality of this malt is very high, and the flavor is much better than that of the foreign malts I've tried. Also, the cost is less, especially when shipping expenses are considered. I have found that the best beers are produced when using Pale Dry malt syrup in combination with a light dried malt extract. Dried malt is available only through wine-makers' supply firms. This malt is not hop-flavored and blends very well with the hop-flavored Blue Ribbon, to make an excellent brew. Buying the malt in extract form is convenient for the home-brewer since the complicated steps of cracking and mashing the barley grains, described in the chapter on commercial procedures, have already been accomplished. You simply pour the malt extracts into your container and dissolve them in water.

There is one very important point I should make concerning the mixing of the malt, which I will again emphasize in the section on procedures. *Do not* bring the water to a boil. You will remember from the section on commercial procedures that the malt was kept at a temperature of 153° F. to allow the diastase enzyme to convert starches to sugar for correct fermentation of the malt. If you allow the water temperature to approach the boiling point, you will upset this sugar conversion and cause it to refix at a stage that will not allow the yeast to convert all the malt sugar to alcohol and carbon dioxide. The temperature of the mixing water must not exceed 153°. Every other book on home-brewing has incorrectly given instructions to boil the malt in the water to dissolve it. This will only guarantee that some of the malt sugar will not be converted. This single bit of misinformation from those who should know better has caused many beginners to become unnecessarily discouraged in their attempts at brewing.

Following is an alphabetical listing of some of the major supermarket chains which carry the Blue Ribbon malt extract. Many other grocery stores and natural-food stores carry this product.

NATIONAL CHAINS

A & P Food Stores
Acme Stores
AG Stores
A-Marts
Clover Farm Stores
Colonial Stores
First National (Finast)
Food Fair
IGA Markets
K-Marts

Kroger Stores
Liberty Markets
Loblaw Markets
National Tea Stores
Piggly Wiggly
Red Owl Markets
Safeway Stores
Super Valu Stores
Winn-Dixie Stores

REGIONAL CHAINS

Albertson's
Alterman Foods
Hinky Dinky Stores
Humpty Dumpty
J C Markets

Milgram Food Stores
Richmond Food Stores
Super Duper Markets
Weingarten Markets

HOPS

This ingredient will not have to be purchased for our main recipes. For those who become experienced in home-brewing and would like to try some variations, I have included some recipes calling for the addition of hops separately. Hops are a pungent herb that flavors beer with a bitter taste to counteract the sweetness of the malt. Hops also act as a preservative and add aroma to the beer. Only the leaves of the female hop plant, *Humulus lupulus,* are used in brewing. The male plant imparts an unpalatable flavor and is even outlawed (except for a few sufficient to fertilize female flowers) in many countries which produce significant quantities of hops for brewing. Hops can be purchased in four-ounce compressed packets through wine-makers' supply firms. The quality of the hops largely determines the overall quality of a beer and especially of an ale. The careful blending of the hops is quite evident in the taste of such distinctive ales as Old Tankard.

FERMENTATION YEAST

The quality of the yeast is also a major factor in determining the quality of the beverage. The yeast available in local stores is not suitable for fermentation, only for baking. You should use dried fermentation yeast, available only through wine-makers' supply firms. It has been cultured specifically for fermentation under scientifically pure laboratory conditions, and it comes in a dried granule form which is easy to use.

You may come across advertisements for various liquid yeasts. These should be avoided. I have ordered several of these and either the yeast has been contaminated and soured or the vials have been broken or damaged during shipment and the contents evaporated. Best to stay with the dried fermentation yeast to insure a consistently excellent ferment. You may hit upon the idea of reclaiming some of the yeast from each batch and storing it for use in succeeding batches. While some people do this, I would not recommend it. With the problems of exposure to air and of establishing a totally sterile environment for storing the extra yeast, the yeast sometimes spoils and the quality is always diminished. If you want to economize a little, the best way is to use only one half of a packet of yeast each time and carefully wrap up the rest. This has no effect on the ferment and you can get two batches from one box of yeast.

ADDITIVES

There are several additives which we mix into the beer at various stages to aid in fermentation or in preserving the quality of the beer.

SALT

This is used to aid in yeast fermentation and also to add to the body of the beer. Most beer recipes call for only two teaspoonfuls of salt per five gallons so there will be no perceptible flavor of salt in the end product.

ACID BLEND

Acid blend aids in fermentation by helping yeast break down the sugars into alcohol and carbon dioxide. Its acidity acts as a vitamin replenishment for the yeast. Acid blend can be purchased in powdered form at a nominal cost from wine-makers' supply firms. One teaspoonful of acid blend is added to every five gallons of beer, making it only a trace element so that no acid taste is imparted to the brew. Some home-brewers use the juice of half a lemon as a substitute for the acid, and this is acceptable; but your results will be much more satisfactory if you use the powdered form.

NUTRIENT

Nutrient is added to the beer mix in the fermenter at the same time as the yeast is added. Yeast uses up many vitamins and minerals during reproduction, as I'm sure we all do, and the nutrient contains replenishments, such as Vitamin B_{12}, to aid the yeast in continuing reproduction. This additive is also available through the wine-makers' suppliers.

FINING POWDER

This substance is added to the beer in very small quantities—only one half teaspoonful per batch is required. It is used to clarify the beer by carrying yeast particles to the bottom.

ASCORBIC ACID

To prevent oxidation due to contact with the air, ascorbic acid is added before bottling. One of the secrets of good brewing is to keep the beer from contact with air during fermentation. Since exposure to air cannot be avoided during the siphoning of the beer into bottles, we have to add one half teaspoonful of ascorbic acid. Along with our other measures, this will insure that we turn out quality batches each time with no variations.

SUGAR

One of the reasons for the rich flavor obtained from the beer recipes in this book is that we use almost no sugar in our brew. As mentioned earlier, the use of sugar, whether of the household variety or dextrose, gives beer a sharp, cidery taste. The malt sugars alone supply the required flavor and alcohol content. We do need to use a small amount of sugar, however, to "prime" or carbonate the beer. This is done just before bottling. Two fifths measuring cup of household white sugar dissolved in some of the beer which has been heated (not boiled) in a saucepan will allow the yeast to work further in the bottle to produce one-fourth percent more alcohol and sufficient carbon dioxide to carbonate the beer to the same extent as the commercial variety. (*See* Figure 7.)

WATER

The quality of the water used is of prime importance in brewing a high-quality beer. Many of the world's best breweries are located in areas where high-quality water is available. Coors beer from Colorado is renowned for its light taste, which is due to the mountain spring water used in it. The makers of Pearl beer, which is produced in San Antonio, Texas, pipe in pure artesian-well water from many miles away to achieve their beer's high quality. You may not be so fortunate as to have access to such excellent water for your brewing. If the tap water in your area has a good taste, go ahead and use it. If it has a decidedly mineral taste, you may want to find a suitable alternative, as any taste in the water is naturally imparted to the beer. If you know of anyone who has well water that is clean and pure-tasting, this will certainly be worth the trouble to acquire. You may have firms in your area, especially if the water from the faucets has a very bad taste, that specialize in delivering pure spring water or treated water to homes and office water coolers. You can arrange with them to fill up your carboy every so often at nominal cost. Another alternative is to purchase a water filter and use the water right out of your faucet. The type to buy is a Polymer Ion Filter. This will filter out ninety-five percent of the minerals (including iron, which hinders good fermentation) and effectively remove undesirable tastes. The unit generally costs less than twenty dollars at scientific or hospital supply firms and lasts for 4,000 gallons, or about twenty years' worth of brewing. This filter is not a mandatory item, and you may not want to go to so much trouble initially to find good water; but later on, when you become more of a perfectionist in your brewing, you may want to put this information to use.

CLEANING

It is very important to keep all your beermaking equipment absolutely clean. This must be done with hot water only. No soap or other detergent must ever come into contact with your containers, brushes, or bottles, because their chemical composition will lower the quality of your beer. It is virtually impossible to rinse off all soaps from your materials. A microscopic film always remains, and this is all that is needed to affect the taste of beer and wine. The same applies to your drinking mugs. Rinse them out with hot water only and stand them upside down to dry. Never use a cloth or anything else to dry them, as it will leave small particles which will affect the head of the beer.

This also applies to your other equipment. It is a good idea to fill your new secondary fermenter halfway with very hot water and a one-pound box of baking soda. Let it sit for several hours, turn it over for another few hours, then pour the solution into the primary fermenter and let it sit awhile. This cleans out the industrial film common to polyethylene. The fermenters should then be thoroughly rinsed out with hot water. Thereafter, a hot-water rinsing immediately after each use (with the hand sprayer on the kitchen sink if you have one) will clean them out sufficiently. The baking-soda rinse should be repeated after every fifth batch to keep the containers fresh. Always store the secondary fermenter on its side, without a cap on the opening. Buy a small hand brush to clean out the hop ring from the primary fermenter after each use. As with the containers, beer bottles should be cleaned out immediately after emptying. Yeast and beer are very hard to remove if given a chance to dry out. Use the hand spray with hot water to rinse out the yeast layer on the bottom of the bottle completely, and then use the bottle brush, while the bottle is full of hot water, to clean out the inside completely. Empty and rinse out once more with the spray and leave upside down to dry. Be sure to store your bottles upside down to prevent any dust from settling in them between fillings. Rinse out your siphon hose immediately after use, or it will become messy on the inside, and if this happens, it cannot be cleaned out.

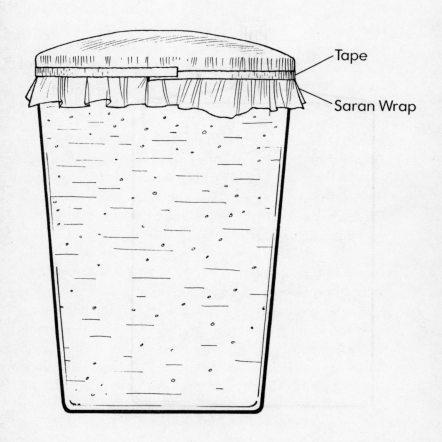

Tape

Saran Wrap

FIGURE 1

Primary fermenter

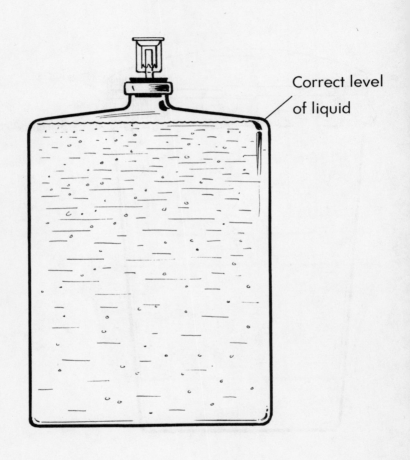

Correct level
of liquid

FIGURE 2

Secondary fermenter (carboy) with fermentation lock attached

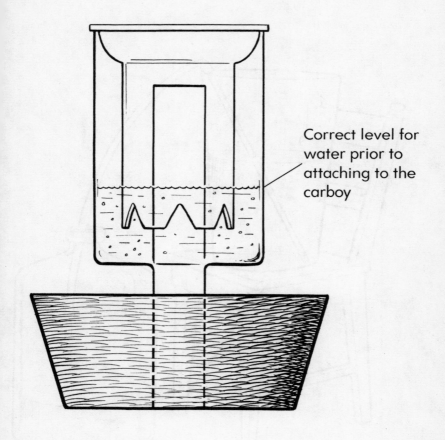

Correct level for water prior to attaching to the carboy

FIGURE 3

Fermentation lock

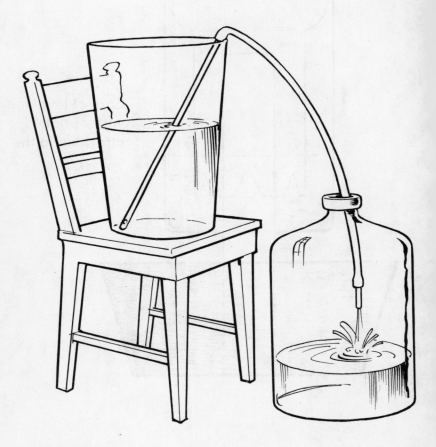

FIGURE 4

Siphoning. To start the flow of beer or wine, suck on the lower end as you would on a straw until the flow is established. The flow end must be kept lower than the drawing end for the flow to continue

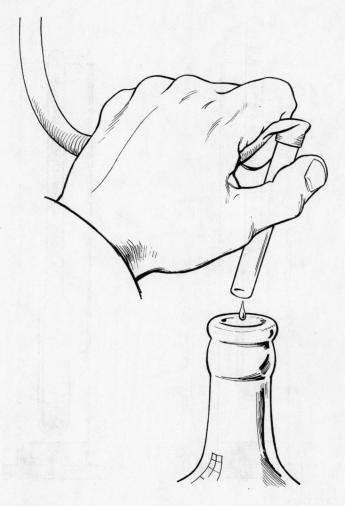

FIGURE 5

Example of how to cut off the flow of siphoning tube to avoid spillage when bottling

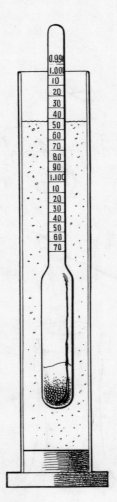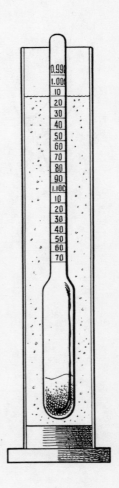

FIGURE 6

Left: *Example of hydrometer reading of 1.042. This is the average specific gravity of beer before yeast is added*

Right: *Hydrometer reading of 1.010—typical level after beer has been two weeks in the carboy. Sugar has almost completely worked out, so that beer is now lighter*

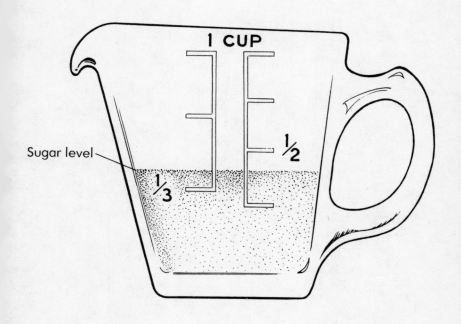

Sugar level

1 CUP

1/2

1/3

FIGURE 7

Since measuring cups do not have a 2/5 level, use a point midway between 1/2 cup and 1/3 cup

Procedure for Beer

Now that you have an understanding of the mechanics of brewing and of the use of the equipment and ingredients, you can proceed to bring all these together to produce a sparkling, rich mug of beer which will impress your family and friends and, most important, yourself.

The first step is to fill the five-gallon secondary fermenter with water to a point one inch below the top. Use the seam of the fermenter as the water line for the correct amount, as it just happens to be an inch from the top. This gives you exactly 5¼ gallons of water, which is the amount called for in all the recipes in this book.* Transfer about

---

* All five-gallon containers—including five-gallon bottles—have a capacity of 5½ gallons. To fill the secondary fermenter completely with the beer mix, use 5¼ gallons of water; the ingredients will take up the other quarter of a gallon.

one gallon of water from the secondary fermenter to the two-gallon mixing pot, heat it to 140° F., and then remove the water from heat. (If you do not have candy thermometer, estimate the temperature.) This is all the heat that is required for your mixing. Mix in one level teaspoonful of acid blend and the amount of salt called for in the particular recipe you are using, and stir. As you will remember, this chemically prepares the water for the correct fermentation of the malt.

Next, add the malt to the pot and stir it until it completely dissolves. If you are making a recipe calling for the use of dried malt along with canned malt, be sure to add the dried malt first and dissolve it completely. If the canned is added first, the dried malt will form lumps when added to the mix and it will take forever to dissolve. You will notice that when canned malt is poured into the pot it sinks to the bottom. This is one reason for removing the pot from the heat before adding the malt. Otherwise, some of the malt would be burned on the bottom of the pan and would impart an unpleasant taste to the beer.

After you have dissolved the malt and stirred the mix for about three minutes, pour the rest of the water from the carboy into the primary fermenter. Then pour the contents of the mixing pot into the primary fermenter and stir in. The total mix should now be cool enough to add the yeast, since only about one fifth of the water was heated. Cut open a yeast packet and stir the contents directly into the primary fermenter. Disregard any directions to mix the yeast before adding it to the beer mix.

This is totally unnecessary and time-consuming. Make sure that the yeast doesn't come into contact with the heated water by itself. Yeast is a living thing and living things do not like to be boiled to death.

Add two teaspoonfuls of yeast nutrient. Some fermentation yeasts contain the nutrient in the same package. This is entirely satisfactory and eliminates the need to add it separately. When the yeast and the nutrient have been added, or "pitched" as the process is known by commercial breweries, cover the fermenter, as shown in Figure 1, with a sheet of extra-wide Saran Wrap and attach a single ribbon of masking or Scotch tape around the top to fasten it tightly.

Cover the fermenter with a towel or dark cloth to keep out the light. You will notice after about thirty hours that the top will begin to billow. This is perfectly normal and is the result of the positive pressure of carbon dioxide gas filling the fermenter from the action of the yeast. This creates an anaerobic environment (one without air), which is desirable in brewing because the bacteria that spoil beer and other foods are mainly airborne. If you look into the fermenter, you will see a rich foamy head bubbling on top. This head is composed mainly of resins from the hops, which are forced up by the carbon dioxide bubbles. Some books advocate skimming off the head, but this should never be done because it contains all the oils and resins that will give the beer its body, aroma, and characteristic beer taste. This head lasts for about a day.

After the head goes back down into the beer, it will

leave behind a hop ring that girdles the edge of the fermenter. This is a gummy and unappetizing-looking substance, but it is pure and harmless and it can easily be cleaned off with a small brush after you have emptied the vessel. One day after the head recedes is the ideal time to transfer the mix to the secondary fermenter, or carboy. First sprinkle one half teaspoonful of finings into one half cup of hot water in a small saucepan and let it sit for ten minutes until it dissolves; then heat to just below boiling to mix the finings completely, stirring continuously. Rinse out the carboy with very hot water to clean it thoroughly. Have the finings solution close at hand before beginning your siphoning. Siphon the beer from the primary fermenter into the carboy. About halfway through the siphoning, add the finings mix; this will insure an even distribution. It is not necessary to interrupt the flow when you add the finings. Try not to spill any of the finings mix on your siphon hose or on the neck of the carboy; it's rather sticky. Be sure that during the siphoning you don't suck up too much of the sediment from the bottom of the fermenter. You will be able to siphon out all but the last half inch or so; this will fill your carboy to the correct height, which is just below the neck. Lift the carboy onto a stool and then fit the fermentation lock, as shown in Figure 2. This lock must be filled with water to the lower line before the cap is inserted. When the cap is inserted and the lock attached to the carboy, place a nickel on the cap to give it extra weight (if it is the loose-top model) and cover the carboy with a towel to keep out the light. Attach a slip of paper to the carboy noting the date, and let the brew work out for fifteen days at normal room temperature—around 70° F.

During this secondary fermentation, the brew will work out to the point where there is little or no sugar left for the yeast to convert to alcohol and carbon dioxide gas. Toward the end of the fifteen-day period, the bubbling in the fermentation lock will slow to about one bubble every ninety seconds or longer. If it is still bubbling at a faster rate than this, let the brew continue to work out for another day or two, then use the hydrometer to be sure it has worked out to approximately the specific gravity indicated for that recipe. When it has, you have reached the bottling stage.

Rinse out the primary fermenter with hot water and drop in one half teaspoonful of ascorbic acid. This will prevent the beer from being affected by contact with the air. Siphon the beer into the primary fermenter, being careful not to disturb the yeast layer on the bottom of the carboy. While siphoning, pour some of the beer into a small saucepan and heat without boiling. Add exactly two fifths level measuring cup of white household sugar (Figure 7) and stir until thoroughly dissolved. Add this sugar solution to the beer in the primary fermenter and mix with a long plastic spoon to insure an even distribution. This is called priming the beer, and it will give us the same degree of carbonation as that in commercial beer. As you may already realize, it is imperative that the beer be allowed to work out for the full fifteen days, or longer if called for, or the sugar content after adding the priming sugar may be higher than necessary. The ideal room temperature for fermentation is between 60° and 70°. If this range is maintained, the fermentation should proceed as indicated. Try not to let the room temperature rise much above 70°. The chance of spoilage, while remote, is increased with a rise in temperature. As for the possibility of having to let the brew work out for more than the fifteen-day period, the only instance I can think of for a slower-than-normal fermentation is if your brewing temperature falls below 60° during the fermentation. In any case, the hydrometer removes all the guesswork.

Have your bottles completely cleaned, rinsed, and ready for use. If they are newly acquired, make sure they have been completely scrubbed out with your bottle brush and very hot water. If you have a dishwasher, it is a good idea to sterilize your bottles in it without detergent. Thereafter, sterilization is not necessary if you rinse them out immediately after emptying and scrub them with the bottle brush.

Siphon the beer from the primary fermenter into the bottles. Note Figure 5 for the method of cutting off the flow. Simply bend the tubing with your thumb. Fill the bottles to the standard height of all bottled beer—about an inch and a half from the top. Press on your reusable caps and tip the bottles upside down to wet the seals. Place them upright in their cartons and store at room temperature for at least fifteen days. On the fifth day after bottling, just to add the professional touch, give each bottle a sharp turn of the wrist clockwise and counter-clockwise to shake loose the small particles of yeast adhering to the side and allow them to settle. When you do this, don't shake the bottle vertically or you will disturb the bottom layer of yeast too much.

Fifteen days after capping, the beer will be carbonated. Before this time it will have a sweet, flat taste and will do no justice to your efforts as a brewer. After the minimum aging period of fifteen days, your beer will be tasty and carbonated. However, the peak flavor is not reached until six weeks have elapsed from the time of bottling. This aging, or lagering, is the period during which the hops and malt flavors mellow and the body develops to its full richness and maturity. You may find, as I have, that after three weeks very little of your beer is left to sample, so you may want to brew enough to have a backlog. There have been occasions when I have served my guests beer that has aged only the minimum time, without telling them that I brewed it myself, and in every case they remarked how much richer it tasted than the beer they had been accustomed to. Some people even prefer fresh beer to fully aged beer. Since you are brewing your beer to suit your own taste, the choice is left to you instead of to the breweries.

Many people wonder why home-brewed beer is so much tastier than commercial beer. The following excerpt on brewing and malting from the 1929 edition of the *Encyclopaedia Britannica* should cast some light on the subject:

There are two main methods of bottling beer. In the first, the older and simpler method, the beer is at a certain age after casking merely run into a bottle, stoppered and stored. During storage a slight fermentation takes place in the bottle and these beers have a sediment due to the yeast thus formed. These are called "naturally conditioned beers." In the second method, beer in bulk is surcharged with carbonic acid gas and filtered into bottles, so that there is no sediment. These are the so-called non-deposit beers; this latter class forms the majority of bottled beers.

Naturally Conditioned Beer. Naturally conditioned beers *form the higher classes of pale ales.* The beer is matured in cask before bottling, and this, with the subsequent fermentation in bottle, *produces a character which is frequently absent from the non-deposit beers.* The production of these beers requires more technical skill in obtaining just the right quantity of gas in the beer as sold. They require more careful pouring out and there is a certain amount of waste. These points militate against their popularity.*

Since we use the procedure that produces a naturally conditioned beer, we reap the reward of having a richer beer, a beer with much more body and flavor. The slight inconvenience of having to pour slowly and of losing a few drops in the bottom of the bottle is a small price to pay for the enjoyment of such good beer.

The section on procedures would not be complete without a discussion of the differences in preparing homebrewed beer and commercial beer. Commercial breweries treat their beer chemically to keep it from being affected by cold temperatures. This process is called, appropriately

* Reprinted from the *Encyclopaedia Britannica* (1929 edition) by permission of the publishers.

enough, chillproofing. It prevents the beer from becoming cloudy when it is cooled to temperatures approaching the freezing point. This procedure is designed to appeal to the eye rather than to the palate, since this clouding over, an enzymatic process, has little effect on the taste. We do not have to bother with chillproofing our beer. For one thing, we don't have to store beer for long periods at very cold temperatures. For another, the process is complicated and expensive. To eliminate the problem of chilling, don't put the beer into the refrigerator until the day you intend to drink it, ideally around five to six hours before drinking.

It is well known among connoisseurs of fine beverages that as much care must be taken in the serving of beer as in the serving of the finest champagnes. Champagne can be served at a wide range of temperatures. The ideal temperature for beer when served is between 38° and 42°.

The choice of mugs is important also. If you do not have suitable beer mugs, you will want to acquire some. They should be made of heavy glass and have either a handle or a stem, so that the warmth of your hand will not be readily transferred to the beer. Beer mugs should be able to accommodate a twelve-ounce bottle of beer and have enough room left over for a foamy head. Ideally, they should be the same temperature as the beer at the moment of pouring. To accomplish this, put your mugs in the refrigerator about an hour before use. Do not freeze them, as this will ruin any beer. Do not use the mugs for any other beverage and don't use soap to clean them. Rather than drying them with a cloth, allow them to drain dry and store them upside down. If you follow these simple guidelines for the correct serving of beer, the end result will be a more satisfying and enjoyable brew. This applies both to the beer you brew yourself and to the beer you buy from the store.

Because of the small yeast deposit on the bottom of each of your beer bottles, you must pour more carefully than you would a commercial brew, so as not to disturb the deposit and cloud the beer. Pour slowly and try not to bubble the beer at the neck of the bottle. This seems tricky at first, but you will soon get the hang of it. Do not return the bottle to an upright position until you have finished pouring. As you notice the yeast coming forward with the last half ounce or so of beer, stop pouring as it approaches the neck and immediately rinse out the bottle. Since the yeast forms a fairly cohesive layer on the bottom of the bottle, very little of the beer is wasted. If you are pouring from quart bottles, be sure to have three of the mugs lined up side by side so you can pour out the contents continuously without having to raise the bottle and billow the yeast. You may occasionally cloud your beer when pouring, but this is no real problem. The yeast cannot hurt you and is indeed quite nutritious. It will not affect the flavor of the beer in any way. The reason for taking so much care in pouring is purely an aesthetic one. I want my brew to look clear and sparkling.

Now that you have read in detail the procedures for brewing your own beer, you will find the procedure outline on the facing page handy as a quick reference to use during the actual brewing operation.

PROCEDURE OUTLINE

INGREDIENTS

5¼ U. S. gallons of water
Blue Ribbon malt (hop-flavored)
Dried malt extract
Salt
Acid blend
Dried fermentation yeast
Nutrient
Fining powder
Ascorbic acid
2/5 cup of sugar

EQUIPMENT

Primary fermenter
Secondary fermenter (carboy)
2-gallon saucepan
Extra-wide Saran Wrap
Masking or Scotch tape
Small saucepan
Siphon hose
Measuring cup
Bottles, caps

1. Fill carboy to 1 inch from top with cold water. Pour 1 gallon of that water into saucepan and heat to 140°, then turn off stove. Add salt, acid blend, malt. (Dried malt first, if called for.) Stir for 3 minutes.
2. Pour remainder of water from carboy into primary fermenter, add beer mix. Add yeast, nutrient, cover with Saran Wrap, and seal with tape.
3. One day after foamy head recedes, siphon into secondary fermenter. Dissolve finings and add during siphoning. Attach fermentation lock.
4. Allow to ferment for 15 days in carboy.
5. Siphon into primary fermenter. Add ½ teaspoon ascorbic acid. Dissolve 2/5 cup of sugar in small saucepan of warm beer, add to the rest of the beer, and mix thoroughly.
6. Siphon into bottles and cap. Tip each bottle upside down once to wet seal.
7. Store upright at room temperature for at least 15 days.

Beer Recipes

Beadlebrew

This recipe is the culmination of three years of effort to produce a beer that has a far richer taste than commercial beer, yet retains the refreshing, thirst-quenching quality inherent in the light lagers. This beer has been widely acclaimed as the best ever tasted by those who have sampled it. I strongly recommend that you use this recipe for your initial batch. It will produce a medium-light lager beer with a rich malt taste.

INGREDIENTS

3-pound package dried light malt extract
1 can Blue Ribbon Pale Dry malt syrup
1 level teaspoon acid blend
2 level teaspoons salt
Final specific gravity 1.010

Follow the procedure outline on page 61. This beer will be ready to drink after fifteen days of storage at room temperature. However, you will most appreciate the flavor after letting some age for six weeks.

NOTE

If you are unable to obtain pale-dry malt and have to use the other varieties, use only ⅔ of a can of malt and one pound of sugar. This is necessary because in all the other varieties—extra pale, light, and dark—the concentration of hop flavor is too high for normal beer tastes. Using a full can would make the beer unpleasantly bitter. The pale dry has a lower concentration of hop flavor and is the ideal variety.

Munich Dark

INGREDIENTS

3-pound package dried dark malt extract
1 can Blue Ribbon Pale Dry
1 level teaspoon acid blend
2½ level teaspoons salt
Final specific gravity 1.010

Follow procedure outline.

ALE

Ale has a slightly different taste than beer due to a difference in the type of yeast used in fermentation. Lager beer is made with bottom-fermenting yeast and ale is made with a top-fermenting variety. The procedure is the same, except that the brew made with ale yeast must be skimmed periodically before being added to the secondary fermenter, because top-fermenting yeast forms a pancake of yeast on top of the brew. If this yeast layer is not skimmed, it would eventually settle to the bottom, and this would give the ale a taste that is described by brewmasters as "yeast-bitten." The brew should be allowed to ferment in the primary fermenter two days longer than usual before being transferred to the secondary fermenter, so that most of the yeast can be skimmed. The taste for ale is usually an acquired one, as opposed to the taste for beer, which is more acceptable to the American palate.

Using Your Own Hops

The previous recipes in this book call for the use of a malt extract which is hop-flavored. The use of this malt eliminates the need for us to spend extra time and money adding our own hops to the brew. After trying the standard recipes, some of you may want to add your own hops so that you can get more variation in your recipes or feel that you played a greater part in creating your fine brew. Over the past few years I have experimented with a number of recipes calling for the addition of hops separately, and there is a slight difference in the taste of beer prepared this way as opposed to preparations using hopped malt. It is only fair to say that it is strictly a matter of personal opinion whether the beer is improved by this added step. Some think beer made with hops added separately has more character, and some can detect no difference. The standard method certainly has the advantage of convenience. However, by using your own hops, you can brew a beer as light in color and taste as the commercial variety, since you can use dried light powdered malt exclusively instead of combining it with malt syrup, which has a slightly heavier taste. The hops can be purchased from the wine-makers' supply firms in compressed bricks weighing four ounces and usually costing less than ninety cents.

PROCEDURE

Before adding the beer mix to the rest of the cold water as described in the standard procedure outline, pour about one half gallon of the water into a large saucepan and bring it to a boil. Add one half teaspoonful of salt. Cut off a length of cheesecloth (extra-wide) so that you end up with a large square. Break off one fourth of the hop brick (one ounce) and separate the leaves onto the cheesecloth. In addition, break off and set aside a half ounce of hops to add directly to the water during the last five minutes of boiling. This will add aroma, which is lost from the rest of the hops during the longer boiling period. Tie the hops into a very loose sack (loose, because the hops will expand considerably when boiled), put the sack in the boiling water, and let the hops simmer for twenty-five minutes. This will allow the flavors of the hops to come out into the water in exactly the same manner as a teabag. When the water has cooled sufficiently, wring out the sack into the saucepan to extract any excess water. Put a square of cheesecloth in a mesh strainer and pour the hop liquid through it into the primary fermenter. This will effectively strain out hop residues and fragments of leaves that escaped from the hop sack.

In the following recipes I have indicated that 1½ ounces of hops are to be used. This will give the beer an average bitter taste, so try this amount first. If you find that it is too mild or too bitter for your taste, you can increase or decrease the amount of hops accordingly. Do not vary the amount more than one ounce at a time, as anything under one ounce will produce a very weak and insipid beer and anything over 2½ ounces will produce an exceedingly bitter brew. Hops are very potent and they have a strong odor. If you have an exhaust fan in your kitchen, I recommend that you turn it on when you are working with hops to prevent their pungency from permeating your household.

Light Lager

This recipe will produce a pale-light beer similar to that available commercially. It will have a more pronounced malt flavor and more body than the commercial variety.

INGREDIENTS

2 *packages (6 pounds) dried light malt extract (Mix in 1½ gallons of water to prevent lumping. Do not stir until second package is poured in)*
2½ *level teaspoons salt*
1½ *level teaspoons acid blend*
3 *tablespoons strong tea (Adds tannin for astringency, which is desirable when using only dried malt)*
1½ *ounces hops*
Final specific gravity 1.010

Follow procedure outline on page 61. Be sure water has cooled to below 80° F. before adding yeast.

Munich Dark

This will produce a dark, rich beer similar to the German variety.

INGREDIENTS

1 *package dried light malt extract*
1 *package dried dark malt extract*
2½ *level teaspoons salt*
1½ *level teaspoons acid blend*
4 *tablespoons strong tea*
1½ *ounces hops*
Final specific gravity 1.010

Follow procedure outline. Be sure water has cooled to below
  80° F. before adding yeast.

Making a Richer Beer

There is a very subtle taste difference between beer brewed with a combination of dried and canned malt and that produced by the finest European breweries. Our own beer has what can only be described as a lighter taste because we are using pure malt extract, whereas the breweries use mash and steep with whole barley grain. These grains have a small amount of insoluble sugar and starches, and the barley grain husks add a flavor of their own. True connoisseurs of beer can detect and appreciate this subtle difference. Those of you who prefer the thicker and richer imported German beer can achieve this character in your own beer by using the following procedure. This is an advanced beermaking procedure and I recommend that you make a batch or two using the procedures under the standard recipe section before proceeding to this added step. This step is best used in conjunction with the first recipe on page 64 and it will produce a delicious, rich, light lager beer.

First obtain some whole-grain malted barley, which comes in three-pound packages, from a wine-makers' supply firm. Do not confuse this with dried malt extract, as these are the actual hard grains of barley, costing about half what dried malt costs. Measure out one pound per five-gallon batch of beer. This barley is used along with the regular ingredients in the recipe and not in place of them. The grains must first be crushed into small bits, but not powdered, or the beer will not clarify satisfactorily. A food blender on slow speed is excellent for this purpose. Pour one third cup of barley at a time into the blender and turn on for about three seconds. This should be sufficient time to break open all the grains. If more than this amount of barley is added at one time, or if it is crushed for a longer period of time, it will be powdered like flour, which may cause the finished beer to have a slight haze. It is important only that all the grains be broken. A coffee grinder is also satisfactory for crushing the grain. Some people use a rolling pin, but this is a very hard way to do it and not worth the time and trouble.

It is best to prepare this part of your mix several hours before mixing the dried and canned malt. As you will see in the procedure below, the grain must be heated and then allowed to cool before being added to the rest of the recipe. If it is added while hot, two of the 5½ gallons of the mix would be heated instead of just one gallon as under the standard procedure. This would make the entire mix too warm for the yeast, and an interesting but aggravating situation would arise. Initially the yeast would begin fermenting earlier due to the heat, but after it was transferred to the carboy, it would slow down to almost complete inactivity for two weeks and then gradually become more lively and finish working out after a total of four weeks in the carboy. The reason for this phenomenon is that the initial generations of yeast are multiplying in a warm beer mix. After the mix cools down, the yeast has to have time to acclimate itself to a cooler environment. The problem is eliminated before it arises by giving the barley-grain mix time to cool in the refrigerator before adding it to the malt mix.

PROCEDURE

Fill the carboy with water to the standard height along the top seam and pour a gallon out into a large saucepan. Keep the rest of the water in the carboy until later, when you mix the standard part of the recipe. Heat the water in the saucepan to between 151° and 155° F. (using a candy thermometer to measure the temperature). This temperature range is critical for converting the starch in the malted barley into fermentable sugar through the action of the diastase enzyme. Be very careful not to exceed the upper limit of this temperature range. Once the proper temperature has been achieved, a low flame on the center of the burner will be enough to sustain it. Next, pour the crushed barley in a circle around the edge of the pan so that not too much is concentrated in the middle where the heat is higher. To obtain the correct temperature of the barley, leave the thermometer attached to the pan with the end touching the ring of grain. Let the mix simmer at 153° for two hours. During the last two or three minutes, agitate the grains with a spoon or eggbeater to dislodge the malt sugars still adhering to the grains. Bring the solution to a boil, then turn off the stove. When the liquid has cooled to below 90°, pour it into the primary fermenter through a strainer containing a double layer of cheesecloth. Hold back the grains with a spoon if necessary to prevent them from falling out. Add some more water to the grains in the pan, stir, and strain again into the primary fermenter. This is known as "sparging" and it simply rinses more of the malt sugars from the grains to be used in your brew. Proceed with the standard recipe and procedure outline.

The final specific gravity of this beer may be as much as .003 higher than that of the standard recipe. For instance, it may be 1.013 before the priming sugar is added. Since this increase represents some insoluble starches and sugars, it is still safe to bottle after the priming sugar is added. The beer should be aged for three weeks before sampling. After two weeks of storage, you will notice a slight trace of substance floating on top of the beer in each bottle. This is only barley residue and it will sink to the bottom when the neck of each bottle is shaken back and forth a few times.

Again, this procedure is a great deal more time-consuming than the standard recipes. I recommend it only for the serious hobbyist with a taste for European-type beer.

Home-Brew Recipes

The following recipes are similar to those used for years by home-brewers in this country. The main difference between these recipes and all the others in this book is that the home-brew recipes use white household sugar in place of the unhopped malt. The flavor of this beer is not as rich as that of beer made with malt only, and the body is lighter, though many people still prefer it to the commercial variety. In home-brew recipes you have the convenience of being able to purchase the necessary ingredients at your local supermarket. Another advantage to these recipes is low cost. Your outlay for all the ingredients and additives for five gallons will be about what you would pay for one six-pack of commercial beer. Who would ever complain about beer that costs only a few cents a bottle!

Because cane sugar is used in these recipes, the flavor will be slightly cidery. Some people prefer this taste to the lager flavor of beers brewed with malt only. Others prefer the mellow, rich taste of beer brewed without sugar. (If you choose to brew one of these recipes before obtaining powdered malt and you find that the taste is not to your liking, don't let this discourage you. Wait until your dried malt arrives and prepare a batch, using the first recipe on page 64.) These home-brew recipes do mellow if allowed to age longer than the other beers. After six weeks in the bottle, the brew has a far less cidery taste. The recipes for the medium and dark beer will produce a more bitter brew than the pale lager, due to the higher concentration of hop extract in the light and dark malt than in the pale dry. Pale-dry malt has a distinctly lighter and drier taste because corn extract is used in the blending of it.

Pale Lager

INGREDIENTS

1 *can Blue Ribbon Pale Dry*
3 *pounds sugar (One level measuring cup of sugar equals ½ pound)*
1 *level teaspoon acid blend*
3 *level teaspoons salt*
Final specific gravity 1.003

Follow procedure outline.

Medium Lager

INGREDIENTS

⅔ *can Blue Ribbon Light*
4 *pounds sugar*
1 *level teaspoon acid blend*
2 *level teaspoons salt*
Final specific gravity 1.003

Follow procedure outline.

Dark Beer

INGREDIENTS

⅔ *can Blue Ribbon Dark*
4 *pounds sugar*
1 *level teaspoon acid blend*
2 *level teaspoons salt*
Final specific gravity 1.003

Follow procedure outline.

Flavored Beers

After you have made several batches using the standard
beer recipes, you may want to try these recipes, although
probably you would not want to settle on the flavored

beers as a steady drink. They should be considered more a novelty drink, to be served on occasion.

Spruce Beer

This beer is quite popular in Germany and in the Scandinavian countries. The spruce essence used in this beer has a stimulating effect, which gives the beer a refreshing quality and makes it more thirst-quenching. The following recipe will produce a flavor exactly like that of one of the lesser-known German imported beers.

INGREDIENTS

3-pound package dried light malt extract
1 *can Blue Ribbon Pale Dry malt syrup*
1 *level teaspoon acid blend*
2½ level teaspoons salt
1 *level teaspoon of spruce essence (Disregard any recipe that may be included with your spruce essence, as these usually call for a much greater amount of the essence and the resulting beer will taste like camphor!)*
Final specific gravity 1.010

Follow procedure outline. The spruce essence should be added to the mix in the primary fermenter just before the yeast and nutrient are added.

Honey Beer

You may want to try some of this beer to see what our ancestors were drinking. Before the eighteenth century, the English used honey instead of sugar for their beer, as sugar was not available at that time. Honey beer is not to be confused with mead, which is a honey wine. In mead, honey is the primary ingredient. Malt and hops are the primary ingredients in honey beer, the honey being used to increase the alcohol content. In this recipe I have used only half the amount of honey that was used by our ancestors. I think you will find that this is enough to give you a sufficiently strong flavor without its being too overbearing.

INGREDIENTS

1½ *pounds dried light malt extract*
1 *can Blue Ribbon Pale Dry malt syrup*
1½ *pounds of commercial brand-name clover honey (Do not use fresh or noncommercial honey, as this has not been processed and it has a high content of bacteria, which may spoil the beer)*
1 *level teaspoon acid blend*
2 *level teaspoons salt*

Add the honey as you would the malt and follow the standard procedure outline.
Final specific gravity 1.010

Wine Making

Wine making and beermaking are very similar processes. Since the equipment required is identical to brewing equipment and some of the additives are the same as for beer, we can dispense with a description of them, as this has already been adequately covered. The fermentation kit mentioned on page 103 contains the necessary yeast and additives. It will be necessary to obtain only the grape concentrate from a wine-makers' supply firm. Until recently, home wine making was a fairly complicated procedure, as the grapes had to be crushed and the juices extracted and boiled. This was an expensive and time-consuming process that often resulted in spoiled batches because of the wild yeasts and bacteria on the skins of grapes. It is now possible to buy a grape concentrate which has been specifically designed for wine making. The end product is a superb wine with which to stock your cellar.

While the ingredients and procedures shown here will insure high-quality batches each time, you must guard against spoilage by thoroughly cleaning all your equipment before each use. As with beermaking, before you use your fermentation kit for the first time, you should pour a one-pound box of baking soda into the secondary fermenter and fill it halfway with hot water. Let the secondary fermenter sit first on one side and then on the other for several hours. Then shake vigorously and pour the solution into the primary fermenter. This procedure is necessary to remove the slight film present on all new polyethylene containers. Rinse out the secondary fermenter thoroughly with hot water to remove all traces of the baking soda. The primary fermenter can be cleaned more rapidly by filling it with baking soda and scrubbing the entire inside with a small brush.

Until recently, the process for wine making required a period of four to six months from the time of mixing to the point when the wine could be bottled. With the new concentrates and the active wine yeast now available, and using the procedure detailed on the following pages, you will be able to bottle your wine within three to five weeks of mixing the ingredients. As with all wines, your wine will require aging in the bottle before it reaches its peak flavor. This will take six months, but it may be palatable after three months. I strongly recommend that you let it age for the full six months, so that you may see what a truly superb wine you can turn out. The time of aging is compensated for by the fact that a single batch will produce 25 fifth-size bottles, and this should last quite a while unless your friends discover your supply.

There is a wide selection of wine yeasts available for wine making, with separate types for Burgundy, sherry, champagne, etc. However, these types of yeasts tend to be slow starters and slow fermenters. They take three or more days from the time they are added to become active. In wine making, as in beermaking, it is very important to get the fermentation going without too much delay, because the greatest chance of spoilage of the wine is during the period of dormancy before the yeast starts reproducing. The best yeast to use is an all-purpose dried wine yeast that becomes active within a day of adding it to the mix—a Montrachet strain produced by Universal Foods Corp. and available through the wine-makers' supply firms. It is nitrogen packed and absolutely pure. When this yeast is used with the type of concentrate and the procedure described on the following pages, an active and efficient fermentation develops, and the wine will work down to a specific gravity of 1.000 or less in five to ten days during the primary fermentation. With the old methods and ingredients, it would take weeks or months to work out to this point. Formerly, it was necessary to rack, or siphon, the wine off the sediment several times during fermentation to prevent the sediment from contributing

undesirable flavors to the wine. With the procedure outlined on p. 92, racking is unnecessary due to the speed of
the fermentation and to the new superb grape wine concentrate, which has little or no pulp sediment. The only
transferring required is like that in beermaking—from the
primary to the secondary fermenter and back to the primary fermenter before bottling.

You may wonder whether this fast fermentation, which
may take as little as three weeks to complete, will produce
a lower-quality wine. Actually, the reverse is true. Wine
produced in this manner will be superior, for several reasons. First, the chance of spoilage is virtually eliminated
because of the fast ferment and the minimum contact with
air (since the racking steps are not needed). Second, because there is no sediment other than the pure yeast layer,
undesirable flavors are not developed during the fermentation. And finally, under the fast fermentation method, the
wine retains a greater amount of its subtle natural flavors
and aromas, which are sometimes diminished during a
prolonged fermentation through oxidation or by passing
through the fermentation lock with the carbon dioxide
gas. These subtle elements will in time turn a good wine
into a great wine. Contrary to popular belief, the mellow-
ness and the bouquet of great wines are not formed during the primary or secondary fermentation. In wine the
character and bouquet evolve during a third fermentation.
This is the malo-lactic fermentation and it does not begin
until the wine has been sealed in bottles. The wine peaks

in flavor in six months and remains at a peak for over two years.

A word on alcohol content. The quality of a wine is not necessarily dependent on its alcohol content. The next time you go to a store which handles foreign and domestic wines, look at the alcohol content of the most expensive Bordeaux reds. You will see that the average will range from 11 percent to 12.5 percent by volume. Step over to the domestic-wine counter and you will see that the most inexpensive wines are almost uniformly 14 percent. This is not to condemn alcohol content in wines. Indeed, many excellent wines have high percentages of alcohol, and, naturally, dessert wines, such as port and sherry, are fortified to bring the percentage of alcohol to 18 or 20. The point I am making is that 12 percent alcohol is sufficient for a fine wine. The following recipes will produce wine with an alcohol content of 12 percent. If you want to make wine with up to 14 or 15 percent alcohol, it is easy enough to accomplish. Just add more sugar than I indicate in the recipe. I don't recommend that you do this, however. It will not improve the flavor, body, or aroma in the least. It will only give you 2 or 3 percent more alcohol. Moreover, it will increase your fermentation time by several months and make it necessary to rack the wine periodically during the fermentation.

Your wine should be chilled before serving. It can also be served at room temperature—if your room is 60° F., which is the case in Europe. Serving wines at room temperature means having them at 60° at most. In the United States, the average room temperature is about 70° and this is too warm for wine. A serving temperature of 45° to 60° is ideal for enjoying your homemade wines.

Procedure for Wine

The following procedure can be used to make a variety of wines. It will be necessary only to vary the concentrate to make red table wine, ruby cabernet, white table wine, and muscat. Excellent concentrates are made by the Bear Mountain Winery in California and are available through wine-makers' supply firms. The following recipe is for the most popular type of wine. It will produce a red, robust dinner wine. As with the other concentrate flavors, it can be sweetened before serving if you prefer a mellow or sweet wine.

INGREDIENTS

1 *gallon Bear Mountain Red Grape concentrate*
4½ *gallons water*
7 *measuring cups sugar*
6 *level teaspoons acid blend*
4 *level teaspoons nutrient*
Montrachet active dry yeast
Final specific gravity before bottling .993 to .995

Fill the secondary fermenter with cold water to a point three inches from the flat top. Transfer a gallon of that water to a saucepan, heat to just below boiling, and turn off the heat. Add the sugar to the hot water in the saucepan and dissolve. Add the acid blend and nutrient to the primary fermenter, and pour all but a small amount of the remaining water from the carboy into the primary fermenter. Pour the gallon of sugar water into the primary fermenter. Add the concentrate, then swill its container thoroughly with the remaining water from the carboy and pour it into the primary fermenter. This rinsing dislodges the delicate substances and acids that usually settle to the bottom of the concentrate container. They are needed to insure a healthy fermentation. Campden tablets, a sterilizing agent, are used to purify grapes and grape concentrates. They must never be used with the Bear Mountain concentrate, however, as they have already been added at the winery and the addition of any more will prevent fermentation.*

Stir the mix thoroughly with a large spoon and check the specific gravity with your hydrometer. The specific gravity should be approximately 1.087. If it is slightly below that—for instance, 1.080—just dip out some of the mix into a saucepan, add another cup of sugar to it, dissolve the sugar without heating, and pour it back into the primary fermenter. The reading may be lower at times due to variations in the grape sugar content of the various flavors of grape concentrate.

Before you add the Montrachet yeast to the wine mix, the yeast must be reactivated by pouring it into a cup of warm water. This water must be between 105° and 110° F. Do not exceed a temperature of 115° or the yeast will be killed. It is advisable to have a small medical thermometer to determine the water temperature properly. (A candy thermometer is not accurate enough.) Let the yeast activate in the cup of water for fifteen minutes, then stir moderately to dissolve the yeast lumps completely into solution. Pour the yeast water directly down into the wine mix.† Cover the primary fermenter with Saran Wrap and seal with tape. The ideal room tempera-

* Other brands of concentrates may have to be purified. This is done by adding two crushed 5-grain campden tablets per gallon of wine mix and letting the mix sit for twenty-four hours before adding the yeast.

† Do *not* use this procedure for starting yeast when making beer. Other yeasts have different characteristics, and this method of starting, which must be used with Montrachet, will ruin the dried fermentation yeast used in beermaking.

ture throughout the entire fermentation is 70° to 75°. Active fermentation will normally start within twenty-four hours and continue in the tumultuous stage for five to ten days. During this period the specific gravity will work down to 1.000 or lower.

At the end of the tumultuous fermentation, the wine is siphoned into the secondary fermenter. If the wine is transferred before the tumultuous fermentation ends, it will foam up through the lock on the carboy. If the wine is left in the primary fermenter too long, the carbon dioxide gas may dissipate and some oxidation could occur from contact with the air.

Unlike the head which appears in beermaking, the forming and subsiding of a foamy head in wine making is not necessarily an indication that active fermentation is at an end. During the tumultuous stage, the head may form and dissipate several times. The best indicator is the pronounced "fizzing" sound of the carbon dioxide bubbles as they rise to the surface in great numbers. When the top of the primary fermenter no longer billows *and* the fizzing sound has subsided, it may be time to transfer the mix to the carboy. Check the specific gravity if the tumultuous fermentation appears to be over. If the reading is 1.000 or lower, you can siphon the wine into the carboy. If it is appreciably higher—for instance, 1.010—reseal the Saran Wrap tightly with tape and let it work out another day or two.

Before the transfer, pour one half teaspoonful of ascorbic acid into the secondary fermenter and mix the fining solution. Pour about one half cup of warm water into a small saucepan and sprinkle one level teaspoonful of finings onto it. Let it sit for five minutes, then heat to just below boiling while stirring moderately. Halfway through the siphoning, add the fining solution so that an even distribution is assured. If the mix does not quite come to the top of the secondary fermenter, add water until the mix reaches a point just below the neck. It is important to have very little air space in the carboy when making wine. Attach the fermentation lock, and if it is the two-piece type, put a nickel on the top so that the added weight will slow down the evaporation of water from it.

The wine will be ready to bottle when fermentation has ceased and the wine has cleared. If the wine had a gravity of around 1.000 at the time of transfer from the primary fermenter, it should take three to five weeks to finish working out and clear. If the gravity was around .997, it may take only two to three weeks. During the last few days of fermentation, the lock (with a nickel on top) will bubble at a rate of one bubble every two and a half to three hours and finally cease to bubble. After bubbling ceases, let the wine settle for two days to clarify. Do not remove the lock until you are ready to bottle, because prolonged contact of the wine with air may cause some oxidation.

When you are ready to bottle, siphon the wine very carefully off the yeast layer into the primary fermenter, which should contain one level teaspoonful of ascorbic acid.

Siphon from there into fifth-size wine bottles. The best bottles to use are standard screw-top wine bottles. Avoid the ones with cork tops, as these have to be stored on their sides to remain airtight, and homemade wine must be stored upright. The bottles should be of tinted glass, to prevent the wine from being affected by exposure to the light. When the wine is bottled, store it upright at room temperature. It will reach its peak flavor and bouquet after aging for six months.

If you prefer a mellow or sweet wine, it can be enjoyed much sooner, however. In that case, it need only age for six weeks. To sweeten the wine, prepare a sugar solution made up of two parts sugar and one part water. Heat the solution on the stove in a small saucepan and stir until the sugar is completely dissolved. Pour 1½ ounces or nine level teaspoons of the sweetener into an empty fifth-size wine bottle or decanter, and then pour a bottle of the wine into it also. Pour carefully, as you would the beer. There is a slight trace of yeast on the bottom of the bottle, much less than the layer in beer bottles, and you can pour all but the last half inch of wine. Seal the top and shake the bottle vigorously to mix the sweetener and also to remove the slight amount of carbon-dioxide gas in the wine. Loosen the cap to release the gas and repeat the procedure two more times. Removing the gas gives the wine a more mellow flavor. The bottle should then be put in the refrigerator to settle and chill for several hours before serving. This method of sweetening each bottle makes it possible to enjoy a wide variety of wines from the same batch. One and a half ounces of sweetener will make a mellow wine. I have found this to be the most enjoyable type for most occasions. If you find it too dry or too sweet for your tastes, simply adjust the amount of sweetener accordingly. The wine keeps very well in the refrigerator for several days before it begins to referment from the sugar content. I doubt that this problem will arise, in any case. After tasting the wine, you will most likely drink it up well within that time. For dry wine it is best to wait three to six months before drinking, and it should be decanted into another bottle, leaving behind the slight yeast deposit. It should also be shaken after it is transferred, to dissipate the carbon-dioxide gas. This wine, too, keeps very well under refrigeration after being opened, and, of course, there will be no renewed fermentation since no sugar is added for dry wine.

On the next page you will find the procedure outline.

PROCEDURE OUTLINE

INGREDIENTS	EQUIPMENT
4½ U.S. gallons of water	Primary fermenter
1 gallon Bear Mountain concentrate	Secondary fermenter (carboy)
	2-gallon saucepan
7 level cups sugar	Hydrometer, thermometer
6 level teaspoons acid blend	Extra-wide Saran Wrap
4 level teaspoons nutrient	Masking or Scotch tape
Montrachet active dry yeast	Measuring cup
Ascorbic acid	Siphon hose
Fining powder	25 fifth-size bottles, tops

1. Fill carboy to 3 inches from top with cold water.* Pour 1 gallon of that water into saucepan and heat to just below boiling. Pour in sugar and dissolve.
2. Add acid blend and nutrient to primary fermenter. Transfer all but 1 quart of water from carboy to primary fermenter. Pour in the sugar water. Add concentrate, rinse its container with the rest of the water from the carboy and add to mix. Specific gravity should be approximately 1.087.
3. Pour pack of yeast into cup of warm water (105°–110°). After 15 minutes, stir, pour directly down into wine mix. Cover with Saran Wrap, seal with tape. Cover with dark cloth. Allow to ferment until tumultuous fermentation ends.

---

* For those of you who use a 5-gallon bottle for wine making, fill it to a height of 12½ inches for your initial measure of water, and use only 6 level cups of sugar.

4. Add 1 level teaspoon of ascorbic acid to carboy. Transfer wine. Add fining solution during siphoning. Attach lock. Cover with cloth.
5. After lock has ceased bubbling, let wine clear for two days.
6. Siphon wine carefully off yeast layer into primary fermenter containing 1 level teaspoon of ascorbic acid.
7. Siphon into appropriate bottles, seal, store upright at room temperature.

Mead Making

Like beer, mead is a drink whose origins are lost. The ancient Greeks and Romans drank this beverage in great quantities, especially during orgies, since mead was reputed to be a powerful aphrodisiac as well as a delicious, intoxicating brew. It is a drink which has held the highest acclaim of every culture that has produced it. The Greeks considered it the nectar of the gods, and the Anglo-Saxons, not to be outdone, praised it as the drink of kings and thanes. Mead making flourished in England and on the Continent until the late seventeenth century, when sugar from the West Indies came into general use. Honey is a major ingredient in mead, and with the growing popularity of sugar, honey was no longer in demand as a sweetening agent. Production of honey declined and along with it the popularity of mead. This was most unfortunate for those of us who have a taste for this nectar of the gods.

Several different beverages are in the category of true meads. Strictly speaking, mead is made with honey, water, and yeast. This type of mead may take up to a year to ferment and require up to three years to reach its peak flavor. There are other types of mead, just as delicious, which are made with fruits. These are known as melomels, and they require the same amount of time to ferment and age as our wines. The types of melomels which were once made are: pyment, a honey wine produced by a combination of honey and grape juice; hippocras, which is the same as pyment, with spices and herbs added to enhance the flavor; metheglin, made with honey, spices, and herbs; and cyser, made with honey and apple cider. The type of melomel mead which we will make is pyment, or honey wine. It is believed that the ancient Greeks were the first to develop this drink. It is excellent as a dessert wine or as a bedtime cordial, where one can decide for oneself whether there is any merit in the qualities attributed to this beverage by the imbibers of ancient Greece and Rome.

INGREDIENTS

1 *gallon Bear Mountain Red Grape concentrate (or Ruby Cabernet)*
4 *pounds of honey (organic acacia blossom is excellent)*
4½ *gallons water*
6 *level teaspoons acid blend*
4 *level teaspoons nutrient*
Montrachet active dry yeast
Final specific gravity may be slightly higher than for wine recipe

PROCEDURE

Follow the standard procedure outline for wine making on page 92. You are simply using honey in place of sugar. Mix honey in hot water in the same way as the sugar was dissolved. Let it age six weeks after bottling, and sweeten to taste using the procedure in the regular wine section. Melomel mead is much better as a mellow or sweet wine than as a dry wine.

Old-Fashioned Cider

It is appalling to me that people will pay $1.25 for a jug of apple cider and then drink it up before it has been blessed by the kiss of the yeast. Apple cider in its unfermented state ranks with the kiddie drinks and other assorted beverages that fill grocers' shelves. Add a little brewers' yeast or wine yeast to apple cider and you have an entirely different drink. The resulting beverage is delicious, refreshing, slightly carbonated, and even a little alcoholic. It is now in its natural state, and all the good things of life are better in their natural state.

When you first buy apple cider, it is not in its natural state because it is unfermented. Pour out about one quart from a gallon jug to give the foam room to rise. (Later on, you can pour the quart back in to ferment, so save this in the refrigerator.) Obtain a pack of dried all-purpose wine yeast (not bakers' yeast) from a wine-makers' supply firm and add about one quarter teaspoonful to the jug. At normal room temperature, the yeast will become active in about a day. Fit the screw cap on *loosely;* otherwise, you will blow up the jug.

When the head subsides, you can start drinking the cider by pouring right out of the jug as you need it. You should drink up the cider during the first week of active fermentation, as it becomes increasingly less sweet as the yeast works out the sugar. To cool it down after the fermentation becomes active, put the jug in the refrigerator. This will also keep the cider sweet longer. The cider will be mildly carbonated, even though the jug is not sealed, due to the vigorous activity of good fermentation yeast, which will also make the cider cloudy.

Cider is a drink for all seasons, but one should make sure that it is available as the primary beverage served during Thanksgiving and Christmas dinners. This cider should be made up one week before these occasions, as it should be a little dryer when served with dinner. Serve in mugs chilled in the freezer.

The preceding pages of recipes have included all the major varieties of fermented beverages, from light lager beer to sweet cocktail mead. While the recipes listed are those that have the widest appeal, there are literally hundreds of variations of these few recipes. As you become more experienced as a brewer, you will want to try some variations of your own, such as the use of lesser or greater amounts of malt in your brew, or varying the amount of grape concentrate in your wines to produce a lighter or richer taste. One of the great advantages to brewing your own beer and wine is that, with so many recipes to choose from, you will surely come up with a brew that you can call your own. Others who become aware of your brewing skills may decide to try making their own beer and wine. Many communities have started beermaking and wine-making clubs to further the art. As a brewer of your own fine beers and wines, you will soon find that there is great enthusiasm generated when others become aware of your newly acquired skill.

I hope you will find as much enjoyment in this absorbing hobby as I have.

Equipment Supplies

The following components will enable you to prepare all the recipes listed in this book:

1 heavy-duty polyethylene primary fermenter
1 heavy-duty polyethylene secondary fermenter (5½ U.S. gallons)
1 fermentation lock and inert stopper
1 precision fermentation hydrometer and jar
1 siphon hose
1 long-handled bottle brush
dried fermentation yeast
active dry yeast
nutrient
acid blend

ascorbic acid

fining powder

bottle caps, preferably made of reusable high-pressure
polyethylene

For information on obtaining a complete fermentation
kit, write to:

Specialty Products International, Ltd.

Box 784

Chapel Hill

North Carolina 27514

All ingredients, such as grape concentrate and dried
malt extract, and all additives and yeasts, can be ordered
from the supply firms listed on the form included with
the equipment.